WHAT IS COPYWRITING?

The Beginner's Step-By-Step Guide to Master Copywriting for Seo and Social Media Marketing Plus 15 Copywriting Secrets for Your Success

Max Wilson

Table of Contents

Introduction

Before the Internet was developed to what it is right now, writing copies had become reserved for mostly literature, advertising, and mass communication graduates. After all, advertising and marketing during that time were very limited. And only a few businesses could afford to market their products and services.

But now, because the Internet has become a free marketplace, many businesses have sprouted. Advertising has become cheaper. And a lot of opportunities for copywriting have emerged.

Today, anybody with a decent command of the English language (of course, it includes native speakers) who does not even have a diploma related to writing can become a copywriter. You might be one of them.

However, despite copywriting being a free-for-all field, not everyone can earn high enough. Why? It is a profitable vocation, right? Yes. But be reminded that to be capable or deserving of high rates and pay as a copywriter, you must have well-polished writing and advertising skills. And this book will help you with that aspect.

I hope you enjoy reading this book!

Chapter 1.   What Is Copywriting?

The Goals, Aims and Objectives of Copywriting

There are many misconceptions about copywriting and even a lot of confusion about its purpose and place in the writing world. Some of the questions often heard include what is copywriting, what is it for, who benefits from copywriting and how does it differ from other forms of writing?

What Is Copywriting?

Copywriting is providing written text that is used in marketing or advertising efforts. In many cases, copywriters work inside large organizations, corporations or businesses that have advertising departments. Businesses such as public relations firms, large department stores, magazines and marketing firms may hire full-time copywriters for their marketing departments. A copywriter might help in creating taglines, jingles, press releases, billboards or any other types of promotional materials. A copywriter does not have to be employed by a marketing department as some freelancers are who are also very good at copywriting. Copywriting is not just for big business either, businesses of any size can reap the benefits of copywriting.

What Is the Primary Purpose of Copywriting?

The main purpose of copywriting is to provide strategically developed content that is part of a marketing campaign. The copywriter does more than just write content, they produce content that is designed to move the audience to perform some sort of action. This goes beyond simply informing an audience about a product. The primary purpose behind copywriting is to write ad content that engages the audience and the primary purpose behind the mission and message is to get the consumer to take action. This will depend on what type of product or service is being offered through the company the copywriter is writing for.

What Kind of Action Is the Goal of Copywriting?

A good copywriter will provide compelling enough content that the audience will be stimulated to action of some sort. Actions can be from a very broad range from making a phone call, sending an email, visiting a website, making a purchase, downloading materials or making some sort of contact. Reading the content is not the goal – the action is the desired goal of copywriting. In order to achieve this goal copywriters must develop some of the most creative forms of content.

How Does Copywriting Differ from Content Marketing?

Content marketing and copywriting are two terms that are frequently heard among business professionals. In many cases, they have mistakenly been used interchangeably, but they are not the same thing, even though they may have some similarities. Although the two may be used effectively together, there are some distinctions that set them apart. Content marketing's goal is to educate the reader. This type of content is sent out through email campaigns, posted on blogs and even shared in the form of a video. Copywriting is meant to elicit a specific action from a person. The desired action can vary depending on the primary goals but successful copywriting will convince people to take a certain action.

Copywriting or Advertising?

The only people who actually like advertising are those who are involved in advertising. This is one thing that makes copywriting a unique skill. The content cannot read or be presented like just another ad. If it does, consumers will quickly discard it or even ignore it, to begin with. Even though the goal is to elicit an action from the audience, the content should be easy to read, enjoyable as well as elicit a response. The two are not completely separable, as the content is the bulk of advertising to some degree. However, it must connect with the audience, evoke an emotional response or in some way cause them to want to take action.

Is Copywriting Used for Offline Applications?

There is no doubt that we live in a technologically based world; but does that mean that there is no place for offline copywriting? Obviously, there is plenty of room in this world for both digital and non-digital copywriting. With that being said, it is important to note that any offline copywriting does not lessen the importance or take the place of online copywriting. It's just a statement that there is a place for offline content. Even though we live in a day where there are many companies that are completely based online, there are still some that prefer to use offline copywriting to add a more personal touch. Many companies, especially larger ones use a balanced combination that offers them a lot more reach. And having non-digital means like brochures, leaflets, newsletters or flyers can offer yet another platform through which an audience is directed to an online location to obtain a service or a product. Offline copywriting can be used to elicit the action of visiting the company's website or going online to fill out a survey. Its purpose does not change – it still desires a response.

Who Benefits from Copywriting?

There are many benefits for all involved in copywriting. For the business, it can mean establishing a rapport with a targeted audience and in the long run helping to bolster the reputation of the company. It can also help a business reach the very important goal of getting the company's message across to consumers. Ultimately this can mean more revenue for the company and copywriting is a useful tool to achieve this ultimate goal. But the consumer should not be ignored, they are certainly a viable part of any copywriting campaign and without them, it would not be a successful endeavor. The purpose of copywriting is to elicit a response from the target audience, which means that there is some type of benefit for them as well. They may purchase a useful product, support a brand name or otherwise connect with a business that has something of value to be shared with them. Even though copywriting is geared toward building a connection or relationship between consumer and business, everyone can benefit in some fashion from copywriting.

Chapter 2.   The Importance of Persuasion and How to Use It

Part of learning to be a successful copywriter is learning how to be more persuasive. To do this, it's necessary to dig into psychological ideas and understand what makes people tick, and how to motivate them to take action. Being persuasive isn't immoral or bad – it's part of everyday life and how we interact with people. Becoming more persuasive in your copywriting will be an eye-opener, a look into the world of salesmanship and, more generally, how to be persuasive in everyday life.

The power of rhyme

Ideas that rhyme are more persuasive. For example, it's more persuasive to say, "This product is made from great grapes." Is more persuasive than "This product is made from amazing grapes." Of course, this doesn't mean you should be speaking poetically all the time. It does mean that sprinkling in rhymes at key moments of copy can be powerful.

The power of reciprocity

A great way to persuade people to buy from you is to be the first in providing value. This is the principle that content marketing is based off. If you can first solve a small problem for someone, they are more likely to come to you later and pay you to solve a bigger problem. For example, they come to your website to learn how they can clean their car in half the time, they then come to your website to buy car insurance. You've solved a small problem, they feel that they need to reciprocate by paying you for something, so they buy car insurance.

The power of oddness

Things that are bizarre and unusual are more compelling than something bland and ordinary. For example, the tagline "Our laptops are like spaceships for your mind," is more memorable than, "our laptops are fast and good for web browsing." Again, this doesn't mean everything needs to become ridiculous, but as an occasional tool to grab attention and be persuasive, it works.

The power of authority

Ideally, this is someone who is a leader in the field, has qualifications, and a great reputation – all of these things will make their opinion more powerful. When you show this person likes your product, your copywriting becomes more persuasive to the customer.

The power of your peers

As well as people in positions of power, people are largely affected by what people in a similar position to them are doing. The most powerful example of this is when all your friends are doing something, you want to do that thing as well. Practically, you don't know what the friends of the reader are doing, but you can address people in their demographic. For example, if you know most of your clients are 20-25, you can say "20-25-year-olds love our products," then readers in that age range will think "I'm in that demographic, maybe I'll like it too." This is the power of belonging and group identity. Use it mindfully and your copy will be more persuasive.

Take responsibility for negative experiences

It might seem counter-intuitive but being able to take responsibility and own up to a failure will actually make you and/or your business more compelling. Of course, you don't want to create a reputation for being incompetent. But occasionally taking complete responsibility and being able to say "sorry" correctly will help your business to be more persuasive because it is better perceived.

Share learning experiences with your audience

This is similar to the preceding point. Creating a public image of a business that is human and humble will make it more appealing. People don't want to buy from a brand that seems to always be perfect because they know the real world is messy and no one or thing is perfect. A business that takes responsibility, apologizes when appropriate, and makes its learning experiences public is better perceived by its clientele.

Be specific with promises

When selling a product or service, it helps to be very specific in the promises you make. For example, it is better to say, "Lose 6 pounds of fat in 6 weeks with our product" than it is to say, "Lose fat with our product." Specific promises are easier to grasp for the customer and they'll feel more confident in the product. Grey, fuzzy promises are less appealing. Make promises as specific as possible, and also make downsides as specific as possible. For example, minimize the downside by saying "there is a 30-day money-back guarantee" rather than "we have an excellent returns policy." The former gives a clear, definite promise to the customer that they can feel confident in, the latter is less appealing because the customer is more unsure of what they are getting.

Get emotional

People buy when they have their emotions stirred. You want the reader to feel excited by what the product will give them – you want them to feel the crushing downside if they don't get the benefits, you are promising. Do everything you can to push the potential customer to feel strong emotions and push the upside hard whilst antagonizing the customer's fears.

Newness and novelty are powerful

Differentiation in the marketplace is a powerful way to make your product seem better than the competition. If it's the first in the product, that's fantastic. If it isn't the first, make it different, better in some definitive way. Always think about how you can present something as being better and newer. Also, don't be afraid to focus on the unusualness of the product.

Use testimonials

This comes back to minimizing risk. No customer wants to take a risk when they buy a product. So, the more you can ease all their worries, the better. To do this, have multiple, excellent testimonials throughout your marketing.

If in doubt, discount

Emphasizing the cost savings of a product is always a great move. People love a deal. There is nothing new here. Consider the positioning of the product or service in the marketplace. If you have something more premium, perhaps make the price an afterthought. If the product or service is deliberately priced to be competitive, make this prominent in the sales material.

Sell time

As well as cost savings, customers are trying to save time. Therefore, when positioning a product, focus on the ways in which it will save time for the customer. Everyone wants to save time – it's perhaps the most valuable commodity humans have. This means that you'll want to focus on how fast the product is to take effect, and how little time is needed to put it into place. Think "6-minute abs." In this example, "6 minutes" is such a small-time investment it makes the sale a lot easier. We can all imagine finding 6 minutes a day to work out our abs – pushing this aspect of the product makes it highly desirable.

Start and end strong

When you are listing a series of benefits to a customer, it is helpful to start and end with the best. This is so you get their attention initially and push their emotional state at the end, so they choose to buy. This applies to any form of sales text, whether it is an email, article, or landing page. There has to be a hook initially, and there has to be a clear, strong push at the end.

Test what works for your brand

Every brand will have some persuasion techniques they currently rely on more than others. Take note of these and then begin to integrate new ones and add new creative directions for the sales copy. However, you don't want to be doing this in the dark. The best way to proceed with a campaign is to measure results and then double down on what is working. Do A/B testing whenever possible. This simply means trying one mode against another and then choosing the mode that sells more. For example, create two different sales emails to send to your email list. Have one focus more on time savings and the other focuses on cost savings. Send these emails out and then track which email has the best results. You now know which persuasion tactic is better suited to the brand and where to focus in the future. Always be testing. Find what works. Do more of that.

Chapter 3.   Copywriting for Social Media ADS

How Does a Guest Blog Work?

It is fairly common for every writer to run out of ideas after writing for a long time. Companies, as well as established bloggers, who have a lot of fans following them, maybe looking for other bloggers to write original posts for them so that they do not lose out on ranking. Just like how you would rent out space in your own blog for a quoted amount per month, you can approach established bloggers and publishers with a good article that you would like to publish on their website. If they agree to your offer, you can charge them for each guest post that you make on their site.

Getting Started with Guest Blogging

You can get in touch with leading news and opinion websites like *Huffington Post* with ideas for articles. Some bloggers who write guest posts on *Huffington Post* won their gigs by continuous engagement with the site and contributing well-structured and thoughtful responses for each post. They were later contacted by the editor of the website with an offer for a blog idea. If you get lucky with any opinion websites, you can add an article there and place a link to your blog in the short bio section that follows the article.

There are other platforms that connect bloggers with other fellow bloggers who would like to invite guest posts to their blogs. MyBlogGuest.com is one of those platforms.

Things to Remember

If you want to be successful with guest blogging, you need to keep the following points in mind:

- Always produce unique and non-plagiarized content.
- If there is an existing article that bears a similarity with your article, make sure to inform the publisher upfront about how different your article is from that article while also citing similarities that they both have. Honesty can be quite rewarding. Perhaps the publisher will give you a long-term chance as a result.

What Is a Niche Blog?

A niche blog is a blog whose posts are tailored around a highly specific topic. If your blog posts stick to a specific topic to the maximum and have keywords that are also specific to the topic, search engines like Google or Bing will give you a higher page ranking, resulting in your blog being displayed on the first or second page of search engine results.

How to Monetize a Niche Blog?

After successfully creating a niche blog, AdWords and Affiliate Marketing can be the first steps taken to monetize it. If the blog runs successfully for a long time with a good amount of daily traffic, you can start exploring generating more revenue by creating content that can be viewed only after a paid subscription.

There are a lot of blogs out there that are into niche blogging. One such site is Baeldung.com. They have some free as well as paid articles about programming. Introductory tech tutorials for complete beginners are given for free while they provide master classes or a whole set of tutorials for a particular topic like SpringBoot as paid content. This is a good site to learn how to monetize niche blogs.

Sponsored Content

If you have created blogs in a niche that big companies work on, you can reach out to them to post a few sponsored articles that bring those companies to your follower's attention. Most often, companies look for various online bloggers to write reviews about their products. Having a good review boosts the value of the company and its product.

But that does not mean you should pick up every single product or company that works in the same niche and write all positive reviews about them. Though it may look like a great way to increase traffic and augment the page rank, it may reduce the credibility of your blog. So, make sure you vouch for only those products that you have personally used or those that already have a good reputation in the market.

Publish Related Articles on LinkedIn

This is an extension of social media marketing. You can create a related article on LinkedIn and publish it for free with leads to your blog or blog post added in the footnotes of that particular article. If your article is impactful and attracts the attention of your connections on LinkedIn, it will be shared by them.

You can share your blog post in a group that is relevant to your niche. You can also use hashtags to attract more viewers to your blog.

Chapter 4.   Copywriting For Email Marketing and Direct Marketing

How to Apply the Copywriting Techniques to Your Email Marketing

Of all the places you can post your ad copy, email ad copy is possibly the easiest to write considering that this is really where you can just stick to the techniques and you will get consistent results.

Another good thing about using email for advertising, marketing, or selling is that this is the most cost-efficient method you can use to advertise your product or service. It must be cautioned, however, that while email advertisements used to be very effective back when the Internet was just getting popular and email was still the main form of online communication (as opposed to various social media platforms), the same is not necessarily the case at present. Hence, it is upon the copywriter to ensure that all possible measures of ensuring the effectiveness of an email ad campaign are in place. Remember that while the format of email ad copy allows for a longer copy that provides all the details your target audience might need in relation to the product or service you are offering, people nowadays rarely spend a lot of time reading marketing and advertising emails. Hence, it is best if you follow the techniques without being too verbose. Otherwise, you will run the risk of being too boring and dragging, and prompting your target audience to either delete the email, unsubscribe or just straight up ignore it.

The first one is that you should always put yourself in the shoes of your target audience. Ask yourself this: if you were the one receiving the email ad copy you are about to send out, will you read it through? Will it actually convince you to make a purchase? Or will you just be annoyed to have received something so long? Sure, you are the one writing the copy and, of course, you want to make it work, but maintaining a certain level of objectivity in assessing your approach is what will greatly help you in ensuring that you are writing a copy for your target audience will actually want to read.

The second thing to consider is that there is a general benchmark for email marketing in terms of how you should begin to sell. That is, you need to include at least three calls to action in your emails. These calls of action should be in the form of a hyperlink that will redirect them to your sales page or landing page. Remember that no matter how good your email copy is, if your target audience still has to do research just to find out how they can avail themselves of your product or service, then chances are they will not do any research. Your goal should be to direct the traffic further into your sales funnel. You want people to click on your product and you want them to be able to do so right within your ad copy.

The third thing to consider, which is related to the second, is that you want to structure your email in such a way that the three different calls to action are scattered throughout the email. A good rule of thumb is to add a call to action after every part of the copywriting formula you are using. For good measure, you might also want to add a P.S. section at the very bottom of the email to accommodate those who would usually skim to the very end of the email. This way, even if they skip everything, there is still a way for them to learn more about the product or service you are selling by clicking through to your product or service.

Finally, keep the structure of your emails short to keep your target audience engaged.

How to Apply the Techniques to Your Sales Pages

The good news about writing ad copy for sales pages is that, first, you can afford to write longer copy and, second, you can just go ahead with applying the techniques. You don't have to worry so much about having to make modifications in order to accommodate for limits to the length of your message when trying to capture someone's attention initially.

Being able to write a longer ad copy is good because it allows you to really sell your product or service by thoroughly listing all of its amazing features and advantages, as well as by addressing all the concerns that your target consumers might have about to the product or service. Also, since you can really just use the techniques without having to make modifications, writing copy turns out to be more intuitive. That said, if you have no prior experience in copywriting, then you will not be scrambling to figure out what modifications to introduce to the techniques since all that is really left for you to do is to plug in the relevant information about the product or service you are advertising.

If you are writing long-form ads, the best format to use will be the PAS format or the Problem, Agitate, Solution formula. Since you have an opportunity to really go into detail, you can make your ad sound more personalized, as though you have written it with the reader in mind. Since PAS appeals to the emotions of the readers and is really effective when it comes to the application of marketing psychology concepts, it is the more advisable formula to use if you are writing a long-form copy. That said, you can really take the time here to build a narrative that your target audience can relate to. Take the time to build a vivid mental image that will allow them to envision their circumstances vis-à-vis the outcome they will enjoy if they buy the product or service you are selling, advertising, or marketing.

Note, however, that just because you are writing long-form copy does not mean that it has to be boring. If anything, it is even more important to make it as interesting as possible since you do not want your target audience to lose interest in the middle of reading your advertisement. One way to do this is by writing something attention-grabbing right at the get-go. This is especially important for medium to long ad copy for sales pages. After all, people tend to not want to read on if they see that there is a lot for them to read. However, if you start with something interesting, something that stirs their curiosity right off the bat, then they are more likely to stay and continue reading the rest of your ad copy.

Chapter 5. SEO and How to Rank on Google

SEO copywriting includes the techniques that allow the web writer to write texts suitable for search engines, with the purpose of securing a favorable position in the pages of Google. In order to do this, the SEO copywriter must pay attention to the use of keywords, readability, Google meta tags, and the analysis of an SEO Specialist who has conducted keyword research.

Indeed, SEO copywriting is based on an assumption that is now clear to all - writing must be for people and not for search engines. In this way, readers will appreciate the content, and Google, in return, will provide rewards via links. This is the essence of online writing. When you work every day for the web, it seems easy to balance the text with the keywords. There are certain types of work, however, that require more attention. Some texts need a true SEO copywriter, a person who can choose and use the most suitable words.

SEO copywriting is a job that combines online writing with search engine rules. The goal is to get quality web pages, both for people and for Google's spiders, while always having in mind the strategic objectives. It is not just about entering keywords or applying them repeatedly in the text. The same goes for the use of synonyms. In essence, SEO copywriting is balanced text.

Based on this logic, the choice and utilization of keywords have qualitative value. Would this be a good assumption? A good answer would be: SEO copywriting is the piece of a broader strategy. Through a well-defined plan, identify your goals and proceed accordingly.

Creating useful content

SEO copywriting is an attempt to climb the SERP (Search Engine Results Page) with content. This is a task for the copywriter, a person who knows the rules of search engines and online writing. For example, he understands the importance of the title tag for Google and knows that it must be persuasive to attract a user's click.

It is not simply putting keywords in the right places, which anyone can do. It takes much more to dominate a competitive SERP. You have to understand how to write an optimized SEO page. This involves not only pleasing Google but also the readers of the site you are writing for.

You have to work towards positioning on Google's front page. This will require you to have clear ideas and be aware of the objectives. In the foreground, it is necessary to meet the needs of those who read, using the most sought-after words. You also have to go beyond your own intentions. Talk to the people who have commissioned the work and do not be afraid to request information. Try to enter the mind of an average user. What are his questions? What are his needs? To accomplish this, you have to work with qualitative and quantitative data.

This is the collection work addressed in the preceding paragraphs. At the outset, you have to maintain the perspective that writing for the web and doing SEO Copywriting basically means meeting the needs of readers. There are no black hat mysteries and secret techniques. Simply put, if a text is liked by internet users, it will gain Google's favor. The quality of the content directly meets their questions and information needs. This is the real SEO writing technique: satisfy the reader. Always. Also, improve the user's experience.

SEO Copywriting starts with a brainstorming job with colleagues, customers, and potential readers. The first two can be contacted easily; the third, on the other hand, must be intercepted through tools and common sense.

Understanding research intentions

One of the key aspects of SEO copywriting is grasping the intentions of research and then writing content to meet these intentions. How do you put this theory into practice? You must focus on the main types of searches that people use Google for, such as these queries:

- Navigational, when the user wants to go somewhere.

- Transactional, when the user wants to do something.

- Informational, when the user searches for information.

The navigational research calls into question the name of a specific brand and is made by those who already have a precise idea about what they want. Second is the transactional kind that contemplates an action, usually a purchase intention. Finally, there is informational research, that corpus of queries that corresponds to 80% of online searches. The positioning on search engines passes through the work you do on these keywords.

Information research and blogging

Informational inquiries are those questions users ask in Google on how to do something. What does this mean for those who have to think about keywords?

You have to find out the research intentions to do a good job of SEO copywriting and to position yourself in Google. Two of the best ways you can do this is by working with online tools that give you details and figures about the searches of potential readers (what people are looking for on search engines) and following the communities where discussions are developed. In this way, you gather a lot of information. You must then come up with ways to use these results. The SEO copywriter starts from a keyword, from a precise need, and the means to optimize a page to answer a query.

Still, you have to be circumspect in utilizing keywords. Do you know what happens when you exaggerate with keywords? Try to guess – a penalty from Google. This is the worst possible situation for a copywriter. Readability should always be the first point.

Web copywriting: how to write online

You might ask: Is there an existing set of techniques for SEO writing? Actually, the road to follow is simply to define a topic and work on it to deepen the people's interest. The goal is not to enchant Google with magic formulas; rather, it is to create text based on research about people and the information gathered through observation of communities. The text of the web page sees the reader in the middle and should have the following main components.

Page title

This is the H1 tag. It is the element that a viewer sees before he starts to read. To catch the reader's attention and convince him to explore further, it must be as catchy as possible. In this case, a little persuasive copy does not hurt, while incorporating the most important keywords. This is how to write an effective headline.

SEO-friendly URL

A good URL structure, from the SEO point of view, foresees the presence of the main keywords. This is another element that is shown in the SERP and is highlighted when it matches the query.

Paragraphs of the copy

Here, you have to practice your web writing skills to be able to write great content. Comprehensive articles can answer questions related to a specific theme. Your style of writing should be simple but never banal. Avoid wandering from the subject at hand but create connections with related topics.

Subtitles (header)

These have H2, H3, and H4 tags. Paragraph titles help people scan the text and easily find sections they want to focus on. Tags are commonly used for correlates that have a greater search volume, to meet the readers' needs on finding more interesting points.

Chapter 6. The Best Niches to Copywriting for Profit

Do research on the kinds of niches that are booming right now so you will make more money advertising for those niches. Or, you can also opt to research more on the topics/services that you are familiar with so that you can be sure that you know what you are doing and that you can deliver the best results. Some say that learning more about a niche that you are familiar with and focusing on one niche alone is better because your clients will be sure that you know what you are doing and that you will be able to give them a great quality of service.

Here are some examples of the different kinds of markets/niches that you can help out in:

- Financial market (e.g., foreign exchange trading, currency, stocks)

- Self-help market (e.g., psychology, self-help books, motivational books/events)

- Food market (e.g., restaurants, food trucks, food products, supermarkets, groceries)

- Job market (e.g., classified ads, job placements)

- Healthcare (e.g., vitamins, medicine, pharmacies)

- Alternative medicine (e.g., acupuncture, chiropractic, alternative medicines)

- Furniture market (e.g., furniture, upholstery)

- Beauty/toiletries (e.g., tissue paper, toothpaste, brushes, lotions, make-up, perfumes)

- Wine market (e.g., wineries, vineyards, wines, champagnes)

- Home repair/construction/maintenance

- Construction market (e.g., construction jobs/services, construction supplies)

- Education (e.g., schools, universities)

- Baby products

- Senior healthcare

- Travel market (e.g., hotel accommodations, plane tickets, flight information, hotel information, destination weddings)

- Weddings (e.g., wedding expos/conventions, wedding gowns, wedding planners, wedding venues, souvenirs, flowers)

- Flower shops

- Christian market (e.g., Christian weddings, Christian dating, conventions, churches)

How will you know which of these is the right niche/market for you? Consider the following tips:

- **Choose something that interests you or that you are familiar with.** Of course, when it comes to choosing something to work on, you have to choose something that you know much about. When you have an idea about what a subject/topic is about, then things would be easier for you. Plus, when you know what you are talking about and when you love what you are doing, you'll surely be able to do it well.

- **It would be good to go for markets/niches that are booming or flourishing.** Go for something that you like and where the money is, and you'll surely be successful. You have to do some research on market trends, forecasts about the business, and trade processes among others. Plus, if people are talking about the niche or products/services under that niche, then you can be sure that you'll be able to gain some profit.

- **Do copy not just for online companies, but also for brick and mortar (physical) companies.** This way, you're not limiting yourself to just one kind of advertising, and you're not limiting yourself from growing and earning more.

You should also think about these things:

- **Pricing.** Think about how much you'll be asking your clients to pay. If you ask them to pay a lot without doing a great kind of service, chances are they will not come back to hire you again. However, you should not also ask them to pay for very little because this would hurt your integrity and would not compensate for all the effort you'll be putting into the endeavor.

- **Honing your craft.** Learn how to write copy that's smart and witty as well as informative and entertaining all at the same time. If you can write copy like this, then you're on your way to something good.

- **Think about the kind of copy that you will be making.** Think of what you want to offer to people. Are you a Search Engine Optimization (SEO) copywriter or are you going to write copy for print ads or for television? Whatever your services are, be detailed about these and learn how to really do your best so that your clients will always hire your services and will also recommend you to other people.

Remember, before doing anything else, do some research first. This will give you some background about what you are doing and will be able to help you do it well.

Chapter 7.   15 Copywriting Secrets

Plan Your Copy

1. Know the Product

What are you selling?

Every copywriting project starts with the product you're aiming to sell. If you're writing for a company, it's going to be one of these four things:

- A **business-to-consumer product** like orange squash or a microwave
- A **business-to-consumer service** like car insurance or window cleaning
- A **business-to-business product** like a photocopier or a forklift truck
- A **business-to-business service** like accountancy or marketing.

Throughout this book, I use the abbreviations 'B2C' for business-to-consumer and 'B2B' for business-to-business.

You could also be 'selling' something that isn't a purchase, like a charity donation. You'll still be able to use many of the techniques in this book, but your copy will be about how the reader can help someone else, as opposed to helping themselves.

Or you might be 'selling' an idea or an opportunity rather than a product. For example, you might be writing an eBook about information security, to encourage business owners to think more seriously about it. Or you might be writing a job ad, to encourage people to apply. Again, you can still use the same approaches, because you want your reader to 'buy in' to what you're saying, or do something other than making a purchase.

Finally, you might be writing copy that simply offers information. It might be a council leaflet about how to claim housing benefits or a blog post on pruning clematis. In this case, the copy itself is the product, and you 'sell' it by making it as clear and useful as you can.

From now on, to keep things simple, I'm going to call whatever you're writing about 'the product', even though it could be any of the things I've just described.

Understand the product

Whatever the product is, your starting point is to understand it thoroughly. You'll want to think about questions like:

- **What is the product?**
- **What does it do?** How does it work? What problems does it solve?
- **Who uses it?** How do they use it, and when? How does it fit into their lives – at work, at home or elsewhere?
- **Is there anything unusual, or even unique, about the product?** Is it the only one of its types, or is it the best in

some way – fastest, cheapest, most comprehensive? How can that claim be backed up?

- **Why would people buy this product *specifically?*** In other words, what does it offer that rival don't?

- **How do people buy the product?** Where do they have to go, and what do they have to do? Is buying the product quick and easy or long and complicated?

- **Is there a buying journey?** Is the product an impulse buy (like a fizzy drink) or a planned purchase (like a fridge)? If it's planned, how do people go about researching and deciding?

- **What is the product's position in the market?** Is it basic, regular or premium? Is it newly launched or well established? What are its main competitors?

- **Does the product replace something else?** Is there anything that people would have to stop buying, or stop using if they chose this product instead? Why might they resist doing that?

- **What might people buy instead?** The alternative isn't necessarily a direct competitor; it could just be something else they might spend money on. For example, cinemas don't really compete with restaurants, but people might still choose between a cinema ticket and a meal out.

- If the product's already on sale, **what do people think of it?** How is it selling? What press coverage and customer reviews has it got? What about the thoughts of people who sell the product – salespeople, retailers, franchisees, brokers and so on?

- If you're writing about service, **how is it delivered?** Who delivers it? What are their skills, background and personalities, and what does that mean for the customer? Can the customer control or customize the service? Is it completely shaped around their needs?
- Is the product part of a **brand or range?** If so, what rules (written or unwritten) will you need to keep to? How does the brand position itself?
- How do the **history and culture of the company** feed into their product? Is the company an ambitious start-up or an established leader? How is it seen in the market?

These questions could form the basis of a meeting or interview with your client or even a written questionnaire. You might be surprised that they haven't thought about all these things, at least not consciously. If anything, important is still hazy, you need to find it and nail it down – because you can't write about the product otherwise.

2. Know the Benefits

Understand how the features of the product translate into benefits, and which benefits are most important.

Features vs benefits

Imagine we're going on holiday together. You fancy a flashy hotel in Dubai, but I'm yearning for a cozy cottage in the Cotswold. How could I change your mind? Maybe I could tell you lots of interesting facts about my cottage:

- The location is just above the Severn Valley.
- It's got a swimming pool.
- There's a pub just down the road.
- It's got two bedrooms.

To me, those things sound great. But I'm already convinced, while you're actively against my idea. To bring you round to my way of thinking, I need to express the same points in a different way:

- You can sip your morning tea and enjoy the view.
- You can keep up with your fitness program and still have time to relax.
- We can go out for dinner and be home in ten minutes.
- You can sleep in without my snoring disturbing you.

So, what's the difference between these two lists?

The first list presents the cottage's *features*, while the second highlights its *benefits*. In other words, while the first list talks about the cottage itself, the second talks about how it helps you.

Why benefits matter

There are lots of ways to make your copy interesting, and we'll look at several of them later on. But there's one thing that *everyone* is interested in: themselves. So, the simplest way to get their interest is by offering them benefits. Benefits are the heart of effective copywriting. As long as you're offering your reader a real benefit, clearly expressed, they'll stay with you. On the other hand, if they can't understand the benefit you're offering, or appreciate why it's good for them, they'll walk away.

A big part of planning your copy is deciding which benefits you're going to talk about, and in what order. Some projects, like print ads, might be all about one important benefit. A product description on a website might talk about a few different benefits, but some will still be emphasized more than others.

3. Know Your Reader

Understand the person you're writing for, inside and out. Decide what you want them to know, feel or do when they read your copy.

Who is your reader?

We've looked at the product and identified its benefits. Now it's time to think about the person who's going to buy it.

When you see TV ads or outdoor posters, it might seem that they're broadcast at everybody, in the hope that someone will be interested. In fact, most marketing only speaks to a few of the people who actually see it. And that's completely deliberate.

You can't be all things to all people. If you try to appeal to everybody, you'll end up appealing to nobody. Instead, you should focus on the people who are most likely to appreciate the product and its benefits, because they'll be the easiest to persuade.

To keep things simple, I'm going to call the target of your copy your reader, even though they might hear your words in a TV or radio ad, or see your idea in a design that has no words at all.

As Stephen R. Covey says, if you want to communicate effectively, you should 'seek first to understand, then to be understood. If you don't really know who your reader is, you won't be able to write for them. Or you might end up writing copy to please yourself, or your client. That might get your copy approved, but it won't bring in any extra sales.

4. Write the Brief

Sum up the product, its benefits, your reader and your aims in the brief.

What is the brief?

We've looked at the product, its benefits, the reader and what we want them to do. Now we can bring those things together into a written brief for our copywriting project.

A brief is basically a document that declares what your copy needs to do. It's the mission statement for your copywriting project, helping you know your destination before you set off.

The brief is the yardstick for evaluating your copy. As you write, you can look at your copy and ask yourself, 'Does this answer the brief, or part of the brief?' If it does, great. If it doesn't, either your copy needs to change, or the brief may not be right.

Agreeing to the brief helps you keep your work on track. Copywriting projects can run into problems if the different people involved don't agree on what the copy should be doing. If you sort that out up front, things usually go more smoothly later on.

Who writes the brief?

If you're working directly for the client, they may write you a brief, or they may just have a few ideas jotted down. They may provide nothing at all, expecting you to take the lead. Whatever happens, it's up to you to obtain a usable brief, even if that means writing it yourself and getting the client to approve it.

If you're working through an agency, they may put together a brief on the client's behalf. If not, you should be able to chat the project through with them and get a clear idea of what's required. Or they may ask you to speak to the client directly. Again, it's all good, as long as you get the information you need.

As time goes by, you'll probably be able to hold the brief in your mind without putting it down on paper, particularly on smaller projects. Or you might feel that writing a brief, or even discussing it, just holds up the project when you could be getting on with the writing. But there's no harm in writing down the brief, even if you're working completely alone. It's a very good way to focus your thoughts and mobilize your mental resources.

What goes into a brief?

Here are some things that could go into a copywriting brief, beginning with the essentials and moving on:

Product:

- What is the product?
- Who is it for?
- What does it do?
- How does it work?

- How do people buy and use it?

Benefits:

- How does the product help people?
- What are its most important benefits?

Reader:

- Who are you writing for?
- How do they live?
- What do they want?
- What do they feel?
- What do they know about the product or this type of product?
- Are they using a similar product already?

Aim:

- What do you want the reader to do, think or feel as a result of reading this copy?
- What situation will they be in when they read it?

Format:

- Where will the copy be used? (Sales letter, web page, YouTube video, etc.)
- How long does it need to be? (500 words, 10 pages, 30 seconds, etc.)
- How should it be structured? (Main title, subtitles, sidebars, pullout quotes, calls to action, etc.)

- What other types of content might be involved? (Images, diagrams, video, music, etc.)

Tone:

- Should the copy be serious, light-hearted, emotional, energetic, laid-back, etc.?

Constraints:

- Maximum or minimum length
- Anything that must be included or left out
- Legal issues (regulations on scientific or health claims, prohibited words, trademarks, etc.)
- How this copy needs to fit in with other copy that's already been written or that will be written in the future
- Whether the copy will form part of a campaign so that different ideas along the same lines will be needed in future
- Which countries the copy will appear in (whether in English or translated)
- SEO issues (for example, popular search terms that should feature in headings)
- Brand or tone of voice guidelines

Other background information about:

- The product (development history, use cases, technical specifications, distribution, retail, buying processes, buying channels, marketing strategy)

- The product's market position (price point, offers and discounts, customer perceptions, competitors)
- The target market (size, history, typical customer profile, marketing personas)
- The client (history, current setup, culture, people, values)
- The brand (history, positioning, values)

Project management points:

- Timescales (dates for copy plan, drafts, feedback, final copy, approval)
- Who will provide feedback, and how?
- Who will approve the final copy, and how?
- How the copy will be delivered (usually a Word document, but not always)

These are only suggestions. There's no preset format, structure or length for a brief. It could be a long, formal document that goes into exhaustive detail on all the points above. Or it could be a short exchange of emails. What matters is that you get the information you need, and agree with the aims of the project with the client.

5. The Power of Storytelling

Storytelling is a lot of different things. At its core, storytelling is the use of language and narrative in order to communicate something to an audience. The content of the story itself can be fictional (made up) or factual (using real events, people, and data). Stories themselves can serve multiple purposes as well, such as to explain an idea, deliver a message, or simply be entertaining. Because stories can be quite flexible, let us take a look at what storytelling is and isn't so that we can narrow down the definition.

When it comes to our marketing, we want to ensure that there is useful or insightful information in our stories. *This is because we ultimately want to use our stories to help drive our conversion rates.* Another way of framing the idea of useful information is to say that our stories have a point. There is an idea or concept that they want to get across to the audience. For example, if you run a bakery, then you may want your point to be how delicious your cookies are. You could do this by just writing, "we have the most delicious cookies in town." But that isn't very catchy, is it? A more eye-catching way of doing the same thing would be to write a story about one of your customers, someone who goes out of their way to always visit your bakery when they are in the area, or who even makes special trips to get cookies from you despite living so far away. The point of the story is still that "we have the most delicious cookies in town," but now there is an intriguing story that makes us want to know more. Why is that?

Did you notice the main difference between the simple slogan and the story? It is that we added a character into the mix. Stories revolve around characters. Notice I didn't say, people. There are many stories in which the characters are animals. For example, an animal shelter is much more likely to feature animals as their characters than people. Characters offer readers, someone, to see themselves reflected in and someone to connect to emotionally. **When you are telling stories as a brand, you need to make sure that your characters are your customers.** Since people identify

45

with characters, making a character into a customer helps to make the reader feel like a customer as well.

Another core point of storytelling is the concept of narrative structure. A story begins, progresses to the middle, and then closes with an ending. The best stories offer some form of arc throughout, one in which the character changes. In the bakery example, our customer begins without cookies, travels to get to the shop, and ends with cookies. Tied to the customer getting the cookies is also an emotional element. The character started with a desire, worked to achieve that desire, and then was happy with the outcome. A story with a beginning, middle, and end follows what is called the three-act structure, and it is the most widely used story structure in existence. By following this structure and trying to incorporate an emotional experience into the structure, you create stories that can be followed by any and everyone.

Before we look at what a story is not, there are two important elements left to discuss that tie into storytelling as a brand rather than storytelling as a generalization. Your brand or business is made up of people and values. Storytelling is one of the ways that you can share the motivations and values of the brand and the people who run it. If you were running an organization that helped people fight for equal rights, you wouldn't share stories that showed somebody as being unequal in the end. You may share a story about how somebody was treated unequally, stood up for themselves, and was then treated equally because that shows the journey of achieving what you believe in. When brands share stories, they are also sharing their beliefs. They aren't just writing out a

46

mission statement with their goal, but connecting those beliefs with an emotional experience that sticks with readers long after they have finished reading.

Storytelling also isn't just sending out an advertisement for your merchandise. **Now that so many people have stopped reading newspapers and watching television commercials, brands need to be smarter with their advertising. Rather than just telling someone they should buy your stuff; you now need to provide them value through your marketing.** Since the most effective marketing is now done on social platforms, it is important to understand that people are choosing to come to your brand to see what they say. No one is forced to watch an advertisement as they had been in the past. Value is the key. There any many ways that we can provide people with value in our marketing, but we're focusing on storytelling. *Storytelling provides an emotional experience, which is in and of itself, something of value.* When that emotional experience is coupled with useful information, the value doubles, and people will love it.

It is important to remember the concept of structure in your storytelling. This means that you can't just write a couple of thousand words and put it out into the world and expect it to make a difference. You also don't want to simply show people something cool that happened. While cool things happening to your brand are great to share, sharing them in the form of a story will always lead to better results. It's the difference between telling someone that you graduated from university with honors, versus telling someone about how you grew up in a low-income family that couldn't even dream about sending you to college, which meant that you had to study extra hard to get to the top of your class so that you could secure a full-ride scholarship and make your parents prouder than they ever had been before. Adding context and narrative progression to those cool events turns a boring post into an inspiring story.

No matter what your brand believes in, sells, or provides, there are thousands of stories to be found in your daily interactions and operations. By telling these stories using proper storytelling techniques, you will see your sales multiply. Now that we have a solid understanding of what storytelling is in regards to our brands let's examine more closely the reasons that we tell stories instead of just providing bullet points or data.

Write Your Copy:

6. Write Your Headline

Writing good copy takes practice and discipline, but it also takes something that makes many of us cringe: homework. To write compelling ad copy, you're going to have to look at the project from every angle. Who are you writing for? What do they want to read? What is going to grab their attention? What are the best keywords to include? Should you use a familiar, conversational tone, or is this audience strictly business? The successful copywriter knows the answers to these questions before he or she writes even a single word.

Of course, once the process has begun, every copywriting project should start the same way: with a headline. We can't stress how important the headline is - the success or failure of your copywriting services depends on your ability to craft a headline with a gravity well that could be measured by NASA. Hyperbolic as it may sound, if your reader doesn't make it past the headline, you don't have a reader.

The 3 responsibilities of a Headline

1. **A Headline Should Announce Your Products' Biggest Benefit**
   Unless you attract the reader's attention right up front you can count on your visitors to stop reading in about 3 seconds or less. That's about all the time your headline has to make a difference. That is why your headline must grab the reader's attention by clearly stating the biggest benefit someone will get from reading the rest of your sales letter right away.

2. **A Headline Should Be Powerful Enough to Make Them Want to Read More**
   Your headline should compel your prospect to keep reading the rest of your sales letter on your website. It is definitely important to make a powerful statement about your headline without giving away so much information that someone won't have to read the rest of the message to learn more.

3. A Headline Should Deliver an Entire Mini-Sales Message

If you think about it, you'll see that your headline is really a standalone sales message. It is designed to sell someone wanting to read the body of the message. Readership studies show that 80% of your prospects will read only the headline before deciding whether or not they want to know more.

Secrete Strategies to Create a Magnificent Headlines

Let's take a look at some of the secret strategies that you can use when copywriting to create a magnificent headline that will work like a magnet for your readers.

Size Matters!

It seems like we begin every copywriting guide with this tip, but it bears repeating. If your headline doesn't fit neatly into a Tweet with space for links and hashtags, it's not a successful headline. 90-120 characters are the sweet spot and remember that search engines only index the first 65 characters, so make sure that your headline begins with a bang.

Avoid Ambiguity

Your reader should know what they're getting into before they click your article. If you've stumbled upon a masterful pun or bit of wordplay that may be clever and eye-catching but isn't so clear as to the content of your post, save it for the subhead or body text. Be clever and witty later - the headline is just the hook.

Who Else Wants It?

This is one secret that has been proven to work over and over again, and is one of the fundamental secrets of good headline crafting: use your headline to imply that your subject is already something that others know, use, enjoy, or are otherwise engaging in, and therefore that your reader is missing out on something important by not clicking. "Who Else Wants to Lose 10 Pounds?" Well, *I* certainly do!

Add a Little Mystery

The use of words like "Secret" or "Little-Known Facts" will help draw readers in, as they will believe they're getting information that others aren't aware of. "Buying a House" isn't a compelling headline - but "The Secret to Getting the Best Mortgage Rate" or "Little-Known Facts about Getting Approved for a Home Loan," on the other hand, will draw in readers who are looking for insights they can't find anywhere else. Are you not convinced that it works? Look at the headline for this article one more time. Convinced yet?

Use Numbers

Numbers help to quantify what you're talking about. "Getting a Better Body" is a fine headline, but "Getting a Better Body in 2 Weeks" is better, and "10 Steps to Get a Better Body in 2 Weeks" is better still. With numbers, particularly those 10 and below, readers feel like they know what they're getting into. An article on weight loss is still an article, and today's Internet reader is fickle and wants information in a hurry. 10 tips, on the other hand, sounds easy to scale and simple, and even the most-flighty reader can stick around for a list of 10 items. Second, adding the "in 2 weeks" to the end amplifies your claim and helps you stand out in a field of other articles about similar subjects.

The Speedy Approach

As we've said, readers are fickle. Using the Internet to find answers and solve problems has become second nature to most of us. Websites offer quick answers to virtually any of our questions, from home improvement to healthcare, and good copywriting taps into this mindset. When you write a headline that fills the quick-fix, instant-gratification need, you're going to be honey for the speedy-bee reader. Items like "Get Rid of Carpenter Ants Once and for All" or "The Quickest Way to Get Over a Cold" are almost guaranteed to outperform articles with the same information with a blasé headline.

Amplify It

So, you have a good hook and you've got a decent headline: "10 Ways to Get Rich." Not too bad, but there's some room to grow, and we can amp up your copywriting a bit with the use of some powerful adjectives and bold claims. If "10 Ways to Get Rich" is a decent headline, "10 Ways to Get Filthy Rich in Just One Year" is a fantastic one. Remember the other copywriting rules, though; keep it Tweetable, and don't make promises in your headline that you can't keep in your post.

Crafting Amazing Openings

The second most important part of the ad after the headline is the Opening paragraph.

You'll discover:

- Amazing way to grab attention and force him to keep reading. Plus Make your sales message more readable.

- Keep sentences as short as possible, without sacrificing the clarity or power of the message. Short sentences get read fast and easily. Long first sentences risk losing them. They can become boring.

- You should stick to the same principle as in the headline. You must be sure the first paragraphs of your copy explode interest and curiosity.

Answer the question: Why I should read this?

In the opening paragraph, you want to get your reader's attention to what comes after. You want to arouse so much curiosity in your prospect that he can't help but keep reading. You want to push the prospect forward throughout your copy

In the opening paragraphs, you elaborate problem that your prospect has. Also, you may give him announce why he should read your copy. Further, you appeal to the emotional pain of your prospect.

7. Structure Your Copy

Why structure matters

As we've seen, your copy needs to keep the reader reading. That means not only saying the right things but also saying them in the right order. A good structure lets your argument unfold in the reader's mind in a clear, logical way, never putting a foot wrong. It also makes the reader's experience easier and more enjoyable, so they're more likely to remember your message and act on it.

Make a plan

Although it may be tempting to jump straight into the writing, you'll probably get a better result in less time if you plan your copy first.

First, jot down all the high-level ideas you want to cover. Each one of these will become a paragraph in your final copy. You can put them on scraps of paper or sticky notes, or just type them into a document. Then, once you've got everything down, move the themes around until they look like they'll link up in a logical way.

For longer pieces of writing, you might want to put subheadings in your plan, so you can break it up into broad areas as well as specific themes.

When you're planning, just plan. None of the wording in your plan needs to go into your actual copy. If you get drawn into thinking about words and phrases, write them down somewhere else and bring your attention back to the plan. At this stage, all you're doing is fitting ideas together.

8. Call To Action

Calls to action are short sentences that tell the reader to do something.

You decided your aim – what you want your reader to know, feel or do. Calls to action focus on the 'doing' part. For the reader, they're the gateway from active to passive: from reading, listening or learning to actually do something in the real world. You've made your case, and now it's time for them to take action. As we've seen, that action could be buying a product, but it could also be just getting in touch with the company, or something different like making a donation.

Calls to action normally appear at the end of your copy, wherever that may be: written at the bottom of ads, sales letters and articles, or spoken at the end of broadcast ads. In printed media, they're often marked out visually in some way. That tells readers that the call to action is different from the rest of the copy and that they need to act on it.

Things are slightly different online. Here, many calls to action are links, so the reader responds simply by clicking on them. The text of the link should describe what will happen when the reader clicks it. For example, it should say something like 'Read our white paper on Agile development', not just 'Click here'. If there are lots of different elements to a web page, readers may not read everything in order, so calls to action are often placed in a sidebar or a header to make sure people don't miss them.

Strong calls to action can be powerful, but they're not 'get out of jail free' cards. They won't magically spur the reader into action if you haven't built up a strong case in the rest of your copy. Your call to action should be a gentle nudge that encourages the reader to do something they're pretty much ready to do.

Improve Your Copy

9. Get Creative

What is creativity, and why do you need it?

Telling the reader about benefits is the heart of copywriting. It should always be the first thing you try, and sometimes you may not need to do much more. But at other times, you need something more powerful. You need a splash of creativity.

You know creativity when you see it. But how would you define it? What does creative copywriting actually mean?

In my view, there are three sides to the answer.

The first is being *original*. Creative copy is different from what's around it, or from what people expect. That means readers notice and remember it, where a bland 'me too' message would just get ignored or forgotten. All else being equal, we remember things that stand out, not those that blend in.

Original copy achieves what leading copywriter Steve Harrison calls 'relevant abruption'. It gets in the reader's face with an eye-catching message that they weren't necessarily looking for, but now realize they might be interested in.

The second side is being *witty*: saying something in a clever, interesting or unexpected way. Thoughtful copy makes readers think, too. They see something subtle, intriguing or clever, and that makes them 'lean in' to find out more.

Wit often means making your message less obvious, but more interesting. It's about taking something that's easy to say, or something that's been said many times before, and making it fresh and new. As novelist Joy Williams puts it, it's about 'unexpressing the expressible' – saying something by not saying it.

Witty copy offers readers a deal. Instead of being passively spoon-fed a message, they've got to pay active attention and do a little bit of brainwork. In return, they get a double payoff: the meaning of the copy and the satisfaction of having worked it out. In the title of a famous book, they get 'a smile in the mind'.

Originality grabs attention, but earns respect. Because you invite the reader to work with you on creating meaning, they feel that you and they are on the same level. You didn't talk down to them, and they responded by engaging with your ideas. Now your equal partners who share an understanding.

Witty doesn't necessarily mean funny. A witty idea might make the reader laugh, but it might just make them smile, nod in recognition or stop and think. On the other hand, some things can be funny without being particularly witty, like slapstick comedy or LOLcat videos. You can still use them, but they might not involve the reader or earn their respect in quite the same way.

Finally, the creative copy is *emotive*. It makes the reader feel something. That feeling could be something pleasant, like fun, excitement, aspiration, security or confidence. It could be something deep, like love, mystery or compassion. Or it could even be something negative, like fear or anxiety.

The emotion your copy evokes could be one that the reader already feels. For example, many ads for baby products appeal strongly to parents' love for their children. Or you could aim to make the reader feel something new like charity ads do by introducing a good cause and making people care about it.

The stronger the reader's emotions, the more likely they are to take your message on board and remember it. They may also associate their feelings with the product, which is why you should be careful about arousing negative emotions.

Originality, wit and emotion are all matters of degree; you can dial them up or down. You can be conservative, mildly original or radically leftfield. You can say it straight, drop in a subtle wordplay or turn an entire ad into a riddle. You can be cold and detached, add a little human interest or go full-on tearjerker. And you can do all these things in different combinations.

Creativity with purpose

At its very best, marketing can tell powerful truths and enrich our culture – *almost* like art. And the best copywriting can hold a mirror to our lives and loves – *almost* like literature. But they can never be *quite* the same, because while art is complete in itself, marketing always has an ulterior motive, whether it admits it or not. Unlike

Monet, marketing is not content just to paint you a beautiful bridge. It has to tempt you across it too.

So, although creative copywriting may be very original, witty or emotive, it isn't any of those things for their own sake. It's about solving a problem in a creative way. If it has any artistic merit, this will be because it rises to that challenge particularly well.

Remember, copywriting is writing with a job to do. And when it comes to being creative, your job has three parts: to *dramatize benefits*, *answer the brief* and *sell the product*.

Dramatizing benefits means bringing them to life and making them as striking and colorful as you can. The examples in this part will show you what that might mean.

Answering the brief means sticking to the plan you made, so you target the right reader and dramatize the right benefits, and work within the constraints of the project.

Lastly, selling the product means exactly what it says. However good your creative idea is, it's still got to be about the product. If you get carried away with your creativity, your copy may be very original, witty or emotive, but it could be selling itself rather than the product.

Bob Levenson, one of the original 'Mad Men' of 1960s Manhattan, suggested a simple test for this. 'If you look at an ad and fall in love with the brilliance of it, try taking the product out of it,' he said. 'If you still love the ad, it's no good. Don't make your ad interesting; make your product interesting.'

To sum it up: creativity means making your copy original, witty or emotive so you can dramatize benefits, answer the brief and sell the product.

10. Find Your Flow

Every copywriter gets stuck sometimes. Here are some ideas for getting moving again.

Just think

When you're under pressure to write something, it's only natural to focus on the output: the words you need to come up with. But just as important as the *input*: the things, ideas and connections that go into your writing.

So, give yourself the chance to think. Get away from your computer, your laptop, your notepad or whatever else you use to write. Get away from distractions too, like your TV, phone or tablet. Go to a quiet space and just think about the brief for ten minutes, without even trying to write anything down.

This is a good approach if you're a very wordy copywriter who likes tinkering with sentences and phrases to get them just so. That's a good talent to have, but when you're looking for ideas, it can tie you up in details when you need to see the big picture. If a big brush is all you have, broad strokes are all you can paint.

Switch it up

Not finding good ideas where you are? Try moving somewhere else. That could mean physically, mentally or both.

60

One simple technique is just to change the venue. Instead of sitting and staring at a screen with gritted teeth, take yourself off somewhere else with a pen and paper. Different sights, sounds, feelings and smells prompt different thoughts. The new venue could be a room in your house, an office breakout space, a café, a park or anywhere.

Another approach is to give your brain some different food. If you sit with a brief for too long, you can get sucked into a spiral of recycling the same thoughts and ideas. Break it up by reading, watching or listening to something completely different. If you're writing about fruit juice, watch some sci-fi. If you're selling yoga courses, listen to some thrash metal. When you come back to the brief, you might find some new ideas waiting for you.

Free your writing

Freewriting is a useful technique if you're feeling really stuck for ideas and just can't move forward. It's a sort of personal brainstorming session.

All you have to do is write (or type) continuously for a set period – say three minutes. You can write about the product, or your experience of trying to write about the product, or just whatever comes into your head at that moment. It really doesn't matter what comes out. Just keep writing.

Freewriting can help to remove mental blocks and let ideas surface from your unconscious mind. It stops you from slipping into editing rather than writing or improving rather than creating. Some writers do a quick burst every morning, as a sort of 'warm-up' for the day's writing.

Engage your unconscious

Have you ever tried and tried to remember the name of an actor or a song, only for it to pop into your head later when you were thinking about something else?

Your unconscious mind can solve a lot of problems for you. But it works in its own way, and at its own pace.

That's the problem with techniques like brainstorming. Yes, teamwork and random connections can throw up interesting new angles. But you're still toiling in an ideas factory, churning out the concepts under time pressure (and peer pressure).

The simplest way to engage your unconscious is just to sleep. Let the problem sink into your mind overnight and see what surfaces in the morning. Keep a pen and paper by your bed just in case.

Since your body and mind are two halves of one whole, physical activity can help too. Go for a walk, a run, a swim or whatever you enjoy. Meditate, if that's your thing. Different movements for your body often lead to different thoughts in your mind.

Work through weaker ideas

As the saying goes, 'Success lies on the far side of failure'. Remember, the good ideas are out there – and sometimes, finding them is a question of moving past the bad ones. The more you can get down on paper, the quicker that process will be.

To take the pressure off completely, you can even focus on having *bad* ideas. Go ahead and write down the worst approaches you can think of, just to get them out of the way. You might be surprised at what comes after them.

As Thomas Edison said, 'I haven't failed. I've just found 10,000 ways that won't work.'

The power of 'yes' and 'no'

Ideas are fragile. Once they're born, they need to be cared for. And they can easily be crushed if someone stamps on them before they've had a chance to grow.

'Yes, and...' is a great technique for developing ideas. Basically, you're only allowed to accept what someone has said and expand on it by responding, 'Yes, and...'. Questioning or shutting down ideas is against the rules, so each idea gets picked up and taken as far as it can go.

Comedians use 'Yes, and...' when they're improvising, to keep their sketch moving forward. The technique is also used in creative brainstorms and business meetings, to encourage people to collaborate and share ideas.

'Yes, and...' is obviously useful when you're working with other people. But you might also need to use it internally, particularly if you have a tendency to self-criticize. 'Yes, and...' is about suspending your disbelief. It gives you the time and space to think ideas through and see their true worth before you start to judge them.

The quickest way to kill an idea is just to say 'no'. But as top creative Gideon Amichay explains, not every 'no' is the same. Sometimes 'no' is actually 'no, comma' – 'No, we don't have the budget', or 'No, there isn't time', or 'No, try something else'. This kind of 'no' can motivate us to try harder or challenge us to take a new direction. 'Resistance is good,' says Gideon. 'Resistance in innovation, in hi-tech, in art, etc. is great... NO is the beginning of a YES.'

You might hear 'no' from your client, an account handler, a creative director or a colleague you share your work with. Or you might hear it from your own inner voice. If so, find the 'no, comma'. Why is this idea wrong? Why won't it work? How does it need to change, or what else needs to change, to make it work?

11. Engage Your Reader

What is engagement?

When digital marketers talk about 'engagement', they sometimes mean getting people to do certain things online, like sharing or liking on social media. But I'm talking about something much broader than that.

When you write engaging copy, you hold a conversation with your reader. You talk to them as an equal – just one person telling another about something they might like. You use their language, but without talking down. You respect their intelligence. You appreciate that they're probably busy, bored or tired, and you remember that they probably didn't ask for your message. Basically, you treat your reader as you'd like to be treated yourself.

64

Talk to your reader

Marketing is a 'one to many' form of communication, and your copy will be read by lots of people (we hope). But it's still good to think of your reader as an individual person rather than a group. Some of the best copy works like a conversation between writer and reader. On the other hand, some of the worst copy has the impersonal feel of one-way communication, like a memo from managers to the workforce.

Check out this bit of copy promoting gym membership.

Members of Flex Gym can make use of a wide range of equipment, including treadmills, steppers and free weights. Regular use of the gym can bring many health benefits, including improved fitness and weight loss, often in a matter of weeks.

It gets the point across, but it's a bit dull. Now here's the same thing, said a different way.

When you join our gym, you'll be able to use all our equipment, from treadmills and steppers to free weights. Visit us regularly and you could get fitter, leaner and healthier within just a few weeks.

The literal meaning of both these is exactly the same, but the second version talks to the reader directly, using 'you' three times, while the first doesn't use it at all. The second one also uses 'our', setting up a relationship between the gym and the reader, and paints a picture of what the reader will do in the future ('join our gym', 'visit us regularly', 'get fitter, leaner and healthier').

Addressing the reader is one of the easiest yet most powerful ways to make your copy engaging. Instead of talking about something 'over there' in a neutral way, you're talking to the reader directly, one to one. That pulls them into your copy, involving them more deeply in what you're saying as if you really were having a conversation.

Most readers will be alone when they read your copy, so address them as an individual, not part of a group. Even if you're targeting a specific demographic, don't say 'Hey, anglers!' or 'Calling all audiophiles' or anything similar. It shatters the sense of a one-on-one conversation.

12. Be Persuasive

To persuade the reader, you must carefully choose arguments that tip their emotional balance, so that the benefits of acting on your message outweigh the benefits of ignoring it. Once you've done that, the reader's thoughts and feelings will be aligned, and they'll be ready to act on your message.

Persuasion with purpose

Persuasion works best when it's aimed at a simple, clearly defined outcome. Tim isn't trying to convert Olly into a fitness fanatic during this one conversation. He just wants him to try wearing a fitness tracker. If that happens, Tim will have succeeded.

In the same way, your persuasive copy doesn't have to transform the reader's worldview. It just has to get them to take the action you identified which is usually trying a product or contacting a firm. For that to happen, the reader doesn't necessarily have to accept every last claim you make or share all the values of the brand. They just have to believe that the product will offer them value.

If the reader's ideas and attitudes change at all, it will probably happen later on, when they actually use the product. Think of your own experience: your deepest beliefs usually come from things you've lived, rather than things you've heard or read.

13. Use Psychology

Work with readers' natural cognitive biases and distortions to change their point of view.

It's all in the mind

We humans are pretty bad at knowing the truth. In fact, our brains suffer from so many distortions, omissions and biases that our perceptions can be completely at odds with reality. We're particularly hopeless when it comes to comparing things like cost, probability and size. But the good news is that you can exploit these loopholes to give your copy some extra traction.

Now, you might feel that some of these approaches cross the line from persuasion to manipulation. I'm just presenting them as options. Whether you use them is up to you.

The endowment effects

The endowment effect is the tendency to overvalue things we already own. If you've ever tried clearing out your garage or attic, you might have felt this effect in action. You haven't touched that old stuff in years, and you certainly wouldn't buy it again today. But because it's *your* stuff, it's hard to let it go.

Here's an example based on that exact situation:

- **Moving home? Short of space?**
- Don't throw out those treasured possessions. Store them securely at *Big Shed* until you can enjoy them again.

Free product samples, time-limited trials, test drives and free-to-play videogames all play on the endowment effect. Once people experience something and become attached to it, they feel it's already theirs. They may not have paid for it, but they have invested their time and attention, which can be just as valuable. Once they've done that, they're more likely to pay real money to keep hold of it.

Loss aversion

Psychologists have found that we prefer avoiding losses to getting gains of the same value.[70] In other words, we hate to lose more than we love to win.

To play on loss aversion, make liberal use of 'your' to emphasize what the reader already has, while pointing out that they could lose it, like this online ad by Squarespace:

- Get your domain before it's gone
- Get it now

Here, 'your domain' is just a domain that the reader might want. It doesn't even exist until they register it. But the threat that someone else will get there first can still feel like a potential loss.

The Forer effects

Psychologist Bertram Forer gave a group of students a personal profile made up of 13 statements and asked them to say how accurate it was. In fact, the 'profile' was exactly the same for all of them. But they still rated the list 4.26/5 for accuracy, on average.

The statements clicked with the students because they were so vague that almost *anyone* could identify with them. For example:

- You have a great need for other people to like and admire you.
- You have a tendency to be critical of yourself.
- At times you have serious doubts as to whether you have made the right decision or done the right thing.

Forer found that the most universal statements began 'At times...'. That's because we don't feel and act exactly the same way in every situation, with our emotions set in stone. Instead, we're constantly moving through different emotional *states*.

We saw how important it is to empathize with the reader. The Forer effect suggests that the best way to do that might be to talk about something they've probably thought or felt *at some point*. For example:

- From time to time, we all buy clothes that never get worn. Our online personal shopper helps you avoid expensive mistakes.

Or:

- Do you sometimes wonder if you're really saving enough for retirement? Use our simple annuity calculator to see what income you can expect.

To trigger the Forer effect, talk about thoughts and emotions the reader might have, using modifiers like 'sometimes', 'occasionally', 'from time to time', 'now and then', 'probably' and so on. Without these words, your statements might sound too blunt – take them out of the examples above and see.

Reframe costs

We looked at how to reframe benefits for a creative effect. You can also use reframing to show the cost of the product in a different context, or from a different perspective. This helps to overcome the reader's price objections – thoughts like 'I can't afford it' or 'It's just too expensive'.

If you just come right out with the price of a product, the reader will immediately compare it with zero, which is the 'cost' of not buying it at all. But if you say some other number first, your reader will compare every other number they hear soon afterward with that. This is called 'anchoring' because it anchors their expectations in a certain range. So, if you mention a high price before stating the actual price of the product, readers will think it sounds low:

- While a high-end lawnmower can cost well over £600, the *MerryMo* comes in at a trim of £295.

The 'anchor' number can be almost anything, as long as it's relevant (and not an outright lie). It's not really there for information – just to pull the reader's perceptions upwards.

Bigness bias, which is closely related to anchoring, is when smaller amounts sound less significant next to larger amounts. B2B service providers often use it to put their fees in a particular commercial perspective. For example, here's an angle that an information security consultant might take:

- Our information security health check costs just £995. That's a small price to pay for peace of mind when a data breach could land you with a heavy fine, severe reputational damage and thousands of lost sales.

Here, the reader fills in the big number for themselves, by mentally working out what 'thousands' of lost sales would come to, or the financial impact of 'reputational damage'. As long as the amount they come up with is a lot higher than £995, the copy works. (If it isn't, their business is probably too small to use the service anyway.)

Another very popular technique is to compare the price with something the reader feels is affordable, because they've almost certainly bought it:

- For the price of a cup of coffee each week, you could provide clean drinking water for a family in Africa.

This combines bigness bias and consistency. Bigness bias tells the reader 'This isn't a big cost in terms of your weekly spending', while consistency says 'You're happy to pay for that other affordable thing, so how about this one too?'

You can also encourage the reader to think about costs and benefits more broadly, or over a longer timeframe. Accountants call this 'whole-life cost' or 'total cost of ownership'.

- The *MerryMo* is engineered from high-quality steel parts, so it'll keep on cutting for years, giving you many more mows for your money.

This reminds the reader that spare parts and maintenance are part of the cost of owning a mower, encouraging them to think about it as a long-term investment rather than a one-off cost.

You can divide whole-life costs into tiny fractions, using the familiar but very effective 'pennies per day' technique:

- For as little as £2.50 a day, you can have a fully functioning VOIP exchange for your small office, complete with five phone numbers for dialing in or out.

Finally, you can point to other types of cost-saving that offset the price of the product:

- The *instant* water boiler makes a cuppa in seconds rather than minutes, so your team spends less time waiting for the kettle to boil. Over its lifetime, *InstaHot* will pay for itself many times over in energy savings and productivity gains.

Sunk costs

A sunk cost is money that we've spent and can't get back. We tend to honor sunk costs even when it would make more sense to forget them and move on because we feel we'd be 'wasting' the money we spent before if we did.

Imagine you book a theatre ticket in advance, then fall ill on the day of the performance. You might honor the sunk cost by going to the show even if it makes you feel worse, to avoid 'wasting' the cost of the ticket. In fact, the money is gone no matter what you do, and you'd probably feel better if you stayed in.

You can use sunk costs to promote a product that lets people get more value from something they've already bought. For example:

- If you've invested in high-quality tiles, give them a new lease of life with *Tile-o-Paint*, the cheaper alternative to retiling.

Reactance

If you've ever tried to get a small child ready to leave the house, you already know about reactance. It's the tendency to do the opposite of what we're told, even when it would benefit us to comply.

Reactance plays a big part in political campaigning. If a party can position their policies as a rebellion against somebody – Brussels bureaucrats, the liberal elite, corporate fat cats – they can turn a vote for them into a 'protest'. 'They don't want you to do this' is the message. 'Take back control!'

One way to use reactance is to set up a situation where the reader 'rebels' by buying into your message:

- You might not believe this, but *WireCo* broadband could be five times faster than your current service.

By suggesting that the reader might not believe the benefit, this 'challenges' them to do just that.

Or you could try a more passive, softly-softly approach:

- The benefits of switching to *EnergyCo* are crystal clear. But of course, the final decision is yours.

This is like an inverted call to action: giving the reader permission *not* to act. But because the benefits are 'crystal clear', that obviously wouldn't be the smart play.

Embedded commands

Embedded commands are a neuro-linguistic programming (NLP) technique to use that power in a less obvious way.

An embedded command is a sentence within a sentence, usually formed as an imperative. For example:

- You can <u>visit our showroom</u> any time between 9 am and 5 pm.

The mind tends to latch on to concrete images and disregard the rest. Here, the concrete image in the sentence is the command 'visit

74

our showroom'. Even though it's placed in a setting that's much more permissive ('can', 'any time'), NLP suggests that the reader's main takeaway will be the action you want them to take.

Not everyone accepts the theories of NLP, but this is a technique that you can easily throw in for a potential gain without harming the rest of your copy.

The double bind

A double bind looks like a choice between two alternatives, but in reality, both paths lead to the same place. For example:

- You can order online or drop into our store to browse and buy a selection of our sofas.

The reader has two choices, but both entail a purchase. The idea is to present alternatives at one level (how to purchase) that amount to the same thing at a higher level (make a purchase). In this case, both alternatives are also embedded commands ('order online' and 'drop into our store').

Distinction bias

Distinction bias is the tendency to choose an option that seems different from alternatives that are presented at the same time. Even though we might be happy with a particular option on its own, we might see it differently when it's compared with other things.

In copywriting, this means moving the conversation from the benefits of one product to the contrasts between multiple products. Focus on how the product is different from competitors or alternatives, choosing a frame of comparison that favors the product. For example:

- While most controllers only have three ways to program your heating, *ToastyHome* has five.

Readers should *really* be asking themselves how many programming methods are enough, or whether they even care. But if you frame their decision as a choice between two alternatives, one of which seems worse, they'll tend to choose the 'better' one.

14. Dealing With Feedback

Dealing with client feedback is a big part of being a copywriter. You may feel your copy has hit the target, but before it can be used, your client has to agree. That means understanding and responding to their feedback without losing sight of the aims we've looked at so far.

Get your head right

There are two sides to dealing with feedback. There's the practical side, which involves amending your copy to satisfy your client while still meeting the brief. But there's also an emotional side, which is about hearing direct comments on your work without getting uptight or upset. And that can be a challenge if you've put a lot of work into your copy, or if you feel your ideas are really strong and deserve to be used as they are.

So, it's important to remember that *the feedback is on the work, not you*. You may have put your heart and soul into your copy, but for now, you need to get some distance from it. You and your client are on the same side of the desk, working together to tackle the problem and improve the copy. Once your work is approved, you can identify with it more closely again.

Respect the feedback

We talked about seeing things from the reader's side. When dealing with feedback, you need to take the same approach, but with the client.

Feedback can sometimes be frustrating, or even perplexing. But if you want to move forward, you need to meet the client where they are, and that means listening carefully to what they say and understanding the reasons behind it.

Remember: your client is doing the best they can with the resources they have. They want the project to succeed, just like you do, and they don't gain anything by messing you about for no reason.

It might be that your client hasn't worked with a copywriter that much, so they're unsure how to express their feedback. If so, it's your job as the senior partner to take up the slack and make this creative relationship work.

Read what's written

Feedback is hard to predict. You can produce copy that you feel is great, but your client asks for major changes. Or, despite doing your best, you might end up with something you feel is so-so – but the client loves it.

Therefore, any time and energy you spend trying to anticipate or second-guess feedback is probably wasted. Once your draft goes in, occupy yourself with another project in the meantime, or just get out of the office altogether. Also, try not to interpret silence as disapproval. It usually just means the client is busy with other things.

When the feedback arrives, give yourself time and space to process it. Even if you feel angry, don't fire off a defensive email straight away. Before you do anything, read the feedback slowly and carefully, so you fully understand what the client is saying and you don't start wrestling with what you *think* they've said, or what you expected them to say. Then, once you've properly understood the feedback, you can move on to dealing with it.

Negativity bias means that we give far more weight to negative feedback than positive. If you've ever obsessed over a little remark about your hair or clothes, even though you got loads of compliments on the same day, you'll know what I mean. So, make a conscious effort to acknowledge the positive things the client is saying. If they say something like 'It's mostly great, but we just need a few tweaks,' believe them.

Work through the feedback

Once you've established what feedback you're going to act on, start working through the edits. If the client has provided a list of changes, print it out and tick them off as you go. If there are tracked changes in Word, you can address them one by one. This will give you a good feeling of making progress.

Comments added to a Word document are a good way to explain your thinking to the client right there as they read. You can do this even in your very first draft, but it's also a good idea to reply to the client's own comments or explain how you've decided to act (or not act) on the feedback. Notes in the accompanying email are OK, but they can easily get separated from the copy – for example, if it's circulated among a few different people.

Don't just work on a single version of your copy. At the very least, it's good practice to keep each version you send to the client, so you can track how it's changed over time and how you responded to feedback. If you're working on a single shared document on Google Drive or Dropbox, you may want to save offline backups for your own reference.

If you need to experiment, save a separate version as a 'sandbox' and work on that. If it turns out to be the way forward, great. If it's a dead-end, you can retrace your steps without losing anything. Alternatively, if you need to make big cuts, make a 'trash' document and paste the bits you delete in there, so you can bring them back later on if you need to.

15. Project Tips

Getting started in copywriting does not have to be a big challenge as long as you take the right steps to get it all going. When you are ready to start out your career as a copywriter, make sure to take some of these steps to get going on the right foot!

Be creative

Copywriting is all about being creative. You need to take your ideas and put them to good use to help out your client. You don't need to have all the ideas in place right from the beginning; many clients are going to be able to share some of their ideas and with some research, you will be able to come up with some great ideas as well. But the main idea with copywriting is that you need to come up with creative ways to talk to the customer and to get them to see that your product is something of value to them. Once you are able to do this, you are sure to get a great start working in copywriting.

Avoid copying others

Never go out there and write a copy that is going to plagiarize someone else. This is going to give your company a bad name and can make things difficult in terms of finding another job and for legal issues as well. You need to be unique, and the customer is smart enough to realize when you are ripping off an idea from somewhere else, so be careful with this.

It does not matter what kind of copy you are working with. Whether it is with an advertisement on a billboard or a script that you are writing for the radio or television spot, make sure that you are not taking ideas from others. If you are writing blog posts or a book, write everything in your own words. Not only will copying others get you in trouble, but it also doesn't look good for the company professionally. If the company wanted the words of someone else, they would have hired that person rather than you.

Find a way to help others

The whole point of writing this copy is to help out others. You want to show the customer how they are going to benefit from choosing this one product over another. There are a variety of mediums that you can use to do this, from writing a few short lines for a billboard add to filling out blogs, websites, and even smaller eBooks. But no matter the medium you choose to use; the main message should be about helping out the customer.

Some businesses are too busy saying why their product is great and thinking about other parts of the campaign, that they don't stop to think about how the customer is going to benefit. You are not going to benefit at all if the customer feels that you are insincere or if they aren't feeling some kind of connection to the words that you are writing.

So, your first goal is to find a way to help out others. Take a look at the product that you are trying to sell and determine how you are going to be able to make a copy that shows these benefits. The benefits can be almost anything, from saving time to saving money or making life easier, as long as those are benefits that appeal to your target audience.

Avoid the passive voice

The first person is the best choice when writing in your copy. It makes the copy more interesting, helps to make it more personal, and can avoid issues with adding too many words. Too many times writers fall into the trap of using passive voice and you may not even realize that you are doing it. The best thing to do is to use a grammar checking site, like Grammarly, which can take a look at your document and help you to recognize the differences between active and passive voice.

Stay clean and concise

When it comes to writing your content, you need to make sure that it is concise and clean. Using too many words is a waste of time and will just distract from the original message that you are conveying. When writing your copy, you want to portray the information in as few words as possible because this is easier for the customer to remember.

A good way to start is to just write everything out. Anything that comes to your mind for the copy, just write it out. Once you are done, go through and get rid of the thoughts and words that repeat themselves or the ones that just don't matter to the copy at hand. Once you are pretty happy with the information that is inside of your copy, it is time to move into a deeper look at the information. Go through each sentence and try taking out some of the words; does the sentence still have the same basic meaning? If so, then leave the words out. You may be surprised at how many words you are able to cut out with this method to make the copy more concise and cleaner.

Getting started in copywriting is no easy feat. You want to be able to impress the clients with your skills while also writing copy that is going to sell. Good copywriters are able to make any product sound appealing, whether it is a common everyday use item or something that is brand new. Using some of the tips that are in this chapter, and the rest of the guidebook will help you to reach these goals.

Chapter 8. Copywriting: Do It Yourself or Outsource It

Ever since the cyber workspace has reached the equinox of its success, the online market has been flooded with several freelancing websites. These websites act as a platform where employees and employers can interact with one another and work for each other in a safe environment. These sites maintain the trust and confidence of both the parties and in return, they charge some amount out of each project. Some of the most commonly used websites are as follows:

1. Fiverr

It is a freelance service platform designed especially for entrepreneurs. It provides special features and tools that help the owner find talent in the community of online freelancers. It allows people to work both for a long-term contract and short-term contracts. Whether an employer needs a writer, graphic designer, programmer, advertiser, etc., he can search it easily on the site and hire a suitable candidate with the experience and expertise required for that special project.

The great thing about Fiverr is that it is completely free to join. You sign up and start working. Making a good reputation and dealing with the clients all relies on you. The more effort you put in, the more you will excel. The site only charges to make sure both parties are complying with the agreement. To have access to more helping features of the site, a person can also apply for their premium packages.

What is unique about Fiverr?

Though every freelancing website works for one particular goal, i.e., to bring talent to the clients, each site works differently in the way it manages this process. Here are certain features that make Fiverr unique from the rest.

- Fiverr's use the seller-level system built on customer satisfaction. On-time delivery of work and unique services are important factors. It constantly evaluates the working of a seller and tracks their projects and performance. A seller can only apply for more work if he has already completed the earlier given work. This feature saves both the client and the seller from unwanted trouble.

- It gives a secure channel to communicate. Fiverr is concerned more about the privacy of its clients. So, it has a system of communication where users can exchange files and material without having to worry about cyber interference.

- The system is completely transparent in its functions. It provides all the information to both the buyer and the seller about one another and the project so they can make an informed decision without facing any type of loss. The employer's portfolio allows the seller to access his authenticity and credibility. This trust makes the users apply for more work.

- The payment system on the Fiverr website is also well-protected. All the financial data and statistics are completely secure with the client. Only a user can see and control his transactions.

2. Upwork

Where Fiverr is a performance-based freelance website, Upwork is a cloud-based platform that currently has the largest pool of employers and hirers. It is great for businesses of all sizes, from big projects to small ones. It has made the hiring process easier than ever by simply listing the talent as per the level of skills and the type of niche.

What is unique about Upwork?

1. It features a hassle-free screening system. While you are freelancing, it is hard to predict the nature of the applicant or the client. Without having a personal interaction, both parties cannot maintain a mutual trust, which is a prerequisite for good performance. Upwork provides chat scheduling and a profile browsing system that creates that personal connection. It allows the buyers to interview the seller first and interact with him before setting up the milestones.

2. Coordination is essential while working on the project. So Upwork has provided In-App communication channels. Now,

the user can reach out to the client from the palm of their hands using the Upwork application. This app allows online messaging via text, call, or video calls.

3. The implied billing process is the most desirable feature of this website. You can track the billable time and keep the statistics clear without having any external factors. You can verify the working hours and use the tools to schedule the billings as per desire.

4. The search engine used by Upwork is famous for its reliability. It is backed and supported by good data, algorithms, and science. This mechanism allows the user to filter unwanted offers and reach straight to the client of their liking.

3. Freelancer.com

Next in line is Freelancer.com, which is again a freelance marketplace with a crowdsourcing system. It can connect millions of buyers and sellers in over 247 countries worldwide. It offers specialized plans to use all the basic and premium tools. The website has gained the trust of professionals working in technical, creative, and professional spheres. Here, you can easily place your bid on offers related to writing, accounting, marketing, data entry, software development, or engineering; perhaps any skills of yours can lead you to the person looking for a talent like you. Freelancer.com has subscription plans offered on a monthly and annual basis.

What is unique about Freelancer.com?

1. It has a fuss-free recruitment system that provides a solution to all the problems related to the hiring of clients. When you register at Freelancer.com, you can browse for all the registered employees and check their portfolios to assess their abilities. Similarly, the seller can also search for the portfolios of the employer and place his bid on the project if it seems authentic and reasonable to him.

2. With Freelancer.com, you can also monitor your progress both as an employer or as an employee. It has its own desktop application that uses analytics to state the ongoing progress of the user. In light of those numbers, a person can change his course accordingly.

4. iPro

"Run your business with confidence." This is the slogan the iPro team works for. This online platform allows businesses to grow through retailer and employee interaction. Like other freelancing sites, it also acts as a platform to provide a secure environment for work and transactions. It is user-friendly and allows fast and easy registration in no time. A user can apply for different memberships, gold or silver, according to the number of features he wants to avail.

iPro is not only apt at bringing the contractors and the workers close, but it also works to provide a reasonable technical solution to help you build your online empire successfully. This feature of this website has gained more trust from the users as they get all sorts of guidance through the site.

5. PeoplePerHour

One last website on this list is "PeoplePerHour." It is a freelance marketplace that offers good money to freelancers. It empowers working professionals from all parts of the world. They can excel and earn by working on what they are most passionate about. The site allows a secure connection between professionals and employers, and it offers a number of other tools that help you to manage all sorts of freelancing tasks. It has more or less similar features to Upwork, like in-app messaging, proposals, account management, etc.

There is a whole range of pricing plans you can get benefits from, like monthly payment, quote-based, or one-time payments.

What is unique about PeoplePerHour?

1. The account management system at PeoplePerHour is great. Their team manages everything in an organized manner, from the working of the freelancers to the ongoing active projects. The dashboard option allows users to get all the necessary information about managing the interface.

2. Like Upwork, this website also has escrow protection, which means, once the project is accepted by the seller, the payment is kept in escrow by the site, and after the successful completion of that job, the payment is released into the account of the seller.

3. At PeoplePerHour, a person doesn't have to pay to hire a client. The job postings are free of cost.

Chapter 9.   Who Needs a Copywriter

It is important to understand that there are different types of copywriting and numerous types of copywriters. Both the terms copywriter and copywriting refer to a wide range of specializations and competencies. Although some copywriting branches have similar job descriptions, many of them don't have similar job descriptions. Some of the copywriting tags are stretchy, and the freelance copywriter works in any platform for clients either as a sole business or individual company. A copywriter will have to write content for websites, brochures, press releases, user manuals and presentations.

Some companies employ in-house employees to get the copywriting job done, while others depend on freelance copywriters. Freelance copywriting is performed on a per-job basis, and some companies arrange long-term contracts with freelance copywriting specialists. The freelance copywriter offers a proposal, gets the writing job done, revises the copy, and accepts their invoice. Freelance copywriting demands solid copywriting skills, and a copywriter will have to write long copy for typical web pages. Copywriters are skilled in writing selling copy for web pages and journalistic copy for news websites. An ideal copywriter will have sound knowledge of different business sectors to survive in the copywriting industry. The ability to get client requirements spontaneously is a trait of skilled copywriting aficionados.

Experienced freelance copywriters are maestros in understanding the client's requirements when compared with less experienced copywriters. Some copywriters specialize in writing for a particular industry, such as tourism, construction, and real estate. Copywriters should have skills in project management, internet marketing, and search engine optimization. It is to be kept in mind that these skills take a lot of time to acquire and a majority of the freelance copywriters come from diverse backgrounds. Copywriters usually work in agencies, marketing firms, newspapers, publishing houses, and real estate companies.

Talent and flair for copywriting differentiate a successful copywriting master from an unsuccessful one. Studios, marketing organizations, and public relations firms make use of the services of copywriters. A copywriter will have to work along with search engine optimizers, marketing specialists, and graphic designers. It is learned that copywriters will have to deal with their clients directly in some cases, and agency copywriters will be writing bulk sales copies. Gifted copywriters are skilled in producing creative ideas and top-notch web or print content. Agency copywriters show their impressive works done for national and international clients in their biodata. They might have proved their caliber in writing copy for eminent marketing campaigns, and a freelance copywriter will have to deal with companies on his own.

A freelance copywriter will have a better understanding of ground realities in the business than an in-house copywriter. Big business corporations employ in-house copywriters that are equipped with their own marketing departments. As the in-house copywriter works only for one client, it limits their copywriting opportunities. In-house copywriters will get the unique opportunity to develop the voice of a brand in depth. It is a fact that in-house copywriters will have a closely-knit working relationship with their clients.

The job of an advertising copywriter revolves around writing the content for press, television and other types of advertising. Advertisement copywriting consists of the generation of headlines, taglines, and long-copy advertisements. An ad copywriter will usually spend a great amount of time working on slogans, and it features time taking writing. Advertisement copywriters do creative concepts or brief spells of advertisements as a part of their job. They work with graphic designers or art directors to craft ideas for visual communication. Only creative thinkers can perform well as advertisement copywriters, as it is necessary to come up with original ideas. The success of advertising copywriters is determined by their ability to deliver ideas that sell products. Any advertisement that involves a great amount of copy is called long copy, and the skills required for long copy copywriting are entirely different.

An advertisement copywriter is often a creative genius who comes with original advertisement concepts. They will have to produce the content for websites, sales copy, packaging copy as well as press releases. Long-form copy specialists should have key competencies in structuring content and maintaining superior language standards. A long-form copywriter acts as a visual artist and craftsperson, and the work of a long-form copywriter is about maintaining the right quality level. Many copywriters possess all the skills required to write for online publications and magazines.

One major distinguishing characteristic between copywriting for commercial clients and working for a newspaper is the editorial control vested with publishers. Copywriters will have to submit accurate text when they are working for commercial clients. Website copywriting refers to producing content for websites, and the skills of a website copywriter include designing user experience and ensuring usability. A web copywriter should have good knowledge of SEO (Search Engine Optimization), HTML (Hypertext Markup Language) and CSS (Cascading Style Sheet). Some copywriters are known as ace web copywriters too, and the key skill of copywriting remains the same irrespective of the medium. Generation of web text is referred to as search engine optimization copywriting, and the basic concept of SEO copywriting is entirely different from that of copywriting.

Conclusion

Writing ad copy is not rocket science, but it is not something that everyone knows instinctively how to do properly. If you have never written an ad copy before, then it is extremely necessary that you nail down the basics and understand the reasoning behind the principles so as to be able to write a good copy. Otherwise, you will be wasting both time and resources when you try to advertise and market your product.

If you want to master the skill of writing good ad copy, then you need to understand not only the techniques you can use, but also how to apply and modify the said techniques in order to accommodate different types of platforms you will talk about your product or service. The ad copy you will be using for your Facebook ad will be different from that you will be using on your landing page. The distinctions are important to consider because your target audience has different demands and expectations when it comes to ads depending on what platform they are using, and it is upon you to meet such demands and expectations. Once you accomplish this, you will be in a better position to convince your target audience to check out the product or service you are offering, as well as convincing them to make a purchase.

Of course, mastering these techniques will take some practice but, trust me, you do not have to put in 10,000 hours just to master these techniques. In fact, you can just set aside an entire day to work on the various applications of our copywriting formulas and you should be good to go. Despite the difficulty associated with writing good copy, it is actually quite easy to do so long as you know what you are doing, and have a solid grasp of the psychological principles at work. Once you got these pat-down, you will be writing great copy in no time.

Printed in Great Britain
by Amazon

25680597R00057